This book belongs to:

Immaculate Conception School

With Love & Blessing,

Date:

14-Dec-08

It's never too late to write!

Color My World

Harmony Publications, LLC

Color My World

Written by:

Debbie Mancini-Wilson

Illustrated by:

Jackie Cleary

Layout, Creative Input and Design by:

Tony Esposito

ISBN 13: 978-09787586-0-8
ISBN 10: 0-9787586-0-9

Harmony Publications, LLC.
226 Paul Street
Pittsburgh, Pa. 15211
harmonypublications@hotmail.com

Debbie Mancini-Wilson is available for fundraisers, school visits, library readings and poetry workshops.
Please send requests for information to: harmonypublications@hotmail.com

This book is dedicated
with all my love and appreciation

to

~ **My Mom and Dad** ~
Who filled my life with top quality and a huge quantity of family values;
they gave me intangible blessings and gifts to pass along to my kids.

~ **Stefan and Josh** ~
My kids who accepted those gifts and blessed me with more.
They are truly my inspiration ... they are Stosh.

~ **Dana** ~
My husband, my partner who simply accepts me
and allows me to be! ... What a gift.

And, of course,

~ **Yvonne** ~
Who will always be my role model.

I offer this book, with gratitude to all of you,
from the luckiest woman in the world,

~ Debbie ~

Contents

Contents

Introduction

Color My World is an amazing interactive journey for children of all ages to express your emotions and journal your own thoughts ... right here in the book! Stosh (the main character) begins the excursion immediately by inviting you to finish writing the opening poem and then draw a picture in the space provided. Grab a pen -- those spaces were not meant to be blank for long! Then dig into the Origami Poetry Writer at the end of the book to really show off your creativity!

Oh, and don't forget to check out our interactive website:
www.colormyworld.info for more fun with Stosh!

Welcome!

We've written some poems and drawn pictures to match.

We've created many different moods to catch.

We hope they inspire the artist in you.

We've finished some and left others to do.

Like this one for starters, let's make an example.

This is the one we'll use as a sample.

To what mood does this poem appeal?

Try to use rhymes to tell how you feel.

Draw pictures to make the story complete.

Don't just sit and stare at your feet!

Tell your story, don't be shy...

Go ahead -- give it a try!

Be silly or serious, fun or contrite,

But draw what you feel,

and write, write, write!

We'll start you off with a thought right now.

What would you say to me if you were a cow?

Would you say, Moo?

Or, Who are you?

Would you be curious about me?

Or simply want to let me be?

Tell me right now in words of your own.

How would you finish this poem?

If I were a cow . . .

_____

_____
_____

_____

_____

_____

Remember, Poems don't have to Rhyme.
Try making up fun new words.

(Instructions: draw a picture to go with your poem!)

Name Game

Silly because life's more fun that way

Too crazy to sit still all day

Oh, just my Mom's favorite thing

So off tune whenever I sing

Hilariously funny for no reason at all

Because I'm Stosh, and... well, that's all!

Name Game

(Instructions: use your name to create an acrostic poem)

Print each letter of your name on one of the small lines below, and use that letter to begin each line of your poem about yourself: you don't have to use all the lines if your name does not have that many letters, and you can add more lines if your name is longer than this... and remember, your poem does not have to rhyme.

Color My World

I'm going to color my world with bright shiny hues,
But I ask for your help with some things I confuse.

I think that it's odd the way colors are used --
Like when I'm sad why do they call it the blues?

When I want to have fun, then it is said
I must go and paint the town red.

And when I paint the town red, it's a fun place.
Then when I'm mad, it's the color of my face?

Envy is seen as totally green.
White is pure and even serene.

If black is the color bad guys wear,
Why do good guys have black hair?

Do you see why I'm confused about this?

Perhaps it's something I shouldn't dismiss.

But, I've chosen to forget what the world deems.

I'm coloring my own world, the way I think it seems!

I've chosen colors to paint an array

My expressions, I share with you today.

A rainbow of colors, and words to match

A rainbow of images for you to catch!

Imagine coloring your own world -- your way

Start here, start now -- start right away!

Choose your favorite colors, make them be true.

Let no one else color your world for you!

(Instructions: draw and color a rainbow)

Greener Grass

Patti's hair is curly, but she wishes it was straight.

Jen's hair is straight, yet she thinks Patti's hair is great.

Alex's eyes are a beautiful, deep-dark brown.

But he'd like to have blue eyes like Mark across town.

Mary Jo is tall — almost as tall as a tree.

She wishes she was tiny like her friend Peggy Lee.

They say the grass is always greener on the other side,

And Mom says to wear your traits with pride.

I don't quite know what all that means, or what it has to do

With wanting to be darker-skinned, like my friend Betty Lou!

Other Side

If the grass is always greener 'on the other side,'

then I guess that's where I choose to reside.

'Cause my Mom says we wake up and choose

if each day, we're gonna win or lose.

So, my grass is green, my sky is blue

I'm happy from within . . . How 'bout you?

(Instructions: draw a picture that makes you happy inside)

White Cat

My Dad got a cat for me
And I'm so excited, I just can't see.

So, he took this photo for me to show you
'Cause I'm having trouble describing him, too.

I don't know if he's big; I don't know if he's small
I simply don't know anything about him at all.

I'm feeling really bad that I can't see my own cat!
Please tell me what you think about that.

Picture of my cat

Dad says to use my imagination, but somehow I think this just isn't the norm.
Can you find the white cat drinking milk from a white bowl in a snowstorm?

The Colors Within

I really don't care

'Bout the color of your hair.

I'm not concerned with the color of your skin,

I'd really rather know your colors within.

Here is my desire, if you want to hear it. . .

I want you to show me the color of your spirit.

Quite simple is my goal . . .

I want to see the rainbow of your soul!

(Instructions: draw a picture using all the colors of your soul)

Fightin' The Blues

Dizzle dops
and wizzle wops
    and shiny bizzle boos.
  That's what I see in my mind's eye
when I'm tryin' to fight the blues.

It's the place that I visit,
    it's just where I go
when I want to escape
    any sorrow or woe.

You may think it is strange,
    but I don't really mind.
I'm told everyone has
    a way to unwind.

I do so by closing my eyes
    to the problems I find
and reaching way deep
    inside of my mind.

That's where I create
    a special place to hide
    where wiggly wuds
    and lolly luds
  bloom colorfully, far and wide.

Oh, and the cozy cazee
    and the trallily tree
grow as far as the eye can see.

It's my favorite place
    to pick Mully McGees,
        and I'll share it with you,
but, be kind, if you please.

Dizzle dops
        and
wizzle wops
        and shiny bizzle boos.
    Close your eyes and
    I'll close mine.
Together we will fight the blues!

(Instructions: draw a trallily tree... What's a lolly lud?
    What do shiny bizzle boos look like in your mind's eye?)

Black

Black tastes like
Hard sweet chocolate
Filled with caramel.
Black is friends with
Indigo, uncle of
Purple, and
Brother of brown.
Black is terrified of
White's bright light.
Black is angrier than
A tied up bull,
Yet sadder than
A lonely bird
Song.

Black smells like
Smoke from a fire.
Black creeps up
Quieter than a
Sneaking thief.
Black can be softer
Than a pillow or
Harder than a rock.
Black is darker than
The darkest night.
Black is a crow perched
On your shoulder.
Black is a shadow
Coming out of its hiding
Place.

Black is a heart that
Could be gold, with
Cold blood running bold.
Black is the Ashes
Of a Burnt forest.

By: Josh
Wilson

'The Osh of Stosh'

26

(Instructions: what is your favorite color?

Write a poem about it.)

27

Pick-Pack-Polliwog

I went down to the fishin' hole
To catch myself a fish.
I brought along my fishin' pole
And made myself a wish.

My wish came true to my surprise.
I did not think it would,
But right before my very eyes
There my best friend stood!

I walked home from the fishin' hole.
Although I did not catch a fish,
I grinned down to my very soul
'Cause I fulfilled a wish.

You see,
I went down to the fishin' hole
And closed my eyes real tight.
Made a magic wand of my fishin' pole
And wished with all my might.

Right there at the fishin' hole,

I opened my eyes to see,

Sittin' beside my fishin' pole

My wish was there with me!

And

Pick-pack-polliwog

I brought home a dog

Pick-pack-polliwog

I brought home a dog!

Cartwheel

Have you ever done a handstand
Where your feet reach way up high?
Have you ever done a cartwheel?
If not, I wonder why!

Have you ever _____

_____

_____

_____

(Instructions: finish this poem)

30

Crescent Moon

I wish I could sit on the crescent moon.

It would make the most comfortable seat.

I'd recline in the curve so high in the sky

And freely dangle my feet.

I wish I could sit on the crescent moon.

What a beautiful view there would be.

I'd like to sit on the crescent moon,

And I'd like you to be there with me!

When I sit in a chair
I don't sit on my butt.
When I sit in a chair
I sit on my hair.

When you sit down
Do you face front?
Or when you sit down
Do you turn around?

Some people say I'm a bit odd.
And perhaps I should change my way.
But changing me would be a fraud.
I'd rather stay crazy without applaud.

Our Old Car

Oh my goodness,
Oh my gosh!
Our old car
Just got a wash.

It looks so good,
Hard to recognize.
Wouldn't believe it
If these weren't my eyes!

I'm shocked, I'm stunned,
I just need a minute...
Mom says that's OK,
I'm not allowed in it!

33

Dragon in my Soup

There's a dragon in my soup

I don't think I like him there.

There's a dragon in my soup

And he hasn't got a care.

There's a dragon in my soup

And I don't know why he stays.

There's a dragon in my soup

He's been swimming there for days.

There's a dragon in my soup

Oh, I hope he goes home soon.

There's a dragon in my soup

I think he fell down from the moon.

There's a dragon in my soup
I don't know why he's there.
There's a dragon in my soup
I don't know why I care.

There's a dragon in my soup
He looks a bit lonely to me.
There's a dragon in my soup
I'll let him stay a week ... or three.

There's a dragon in my soup
I think I like his company.
There's a dragon in my soup
I hope he stays right here with me.

There's a dragon in my soup
Yes, there's a dragon in my soup.
Oh, there's a dragon in my soup
I just hope he doesn't poop!

Oyshamunga

I made up a word,
I'll tell you what it means.

I made up a word
That means many things.

The word is 'Oyshamunga'
And I use it when I'm mad.

I use it when I'm frustrated
And even when I'm glad.

You may think that contradicts,
But let me explain.

Oyshamunga is a word
I use again and again.

Its meaning depends on how I use it . . .
Where the accent lies.

It depends on how I say it . . .
And the expression of my eyes.

Try it when you're happy about a great event,
Oyshamunga! you can say, with a smile to be spent.

Or, if you yell it when you're scared,
Show your fear, and pull your hair.

If you shout it real loud at some crazy jerk,
Wrinkling your eyebrows really makes it work.

Or, next time you're angry and throw your hands into the air,
Yelling "Oyshamunga!" really goes well there.

But when your dog snuggles and licks your face,
A gentle, quiet "Oyshamunga!" really fits the space.

Be creative when you yell it,
scream, or whisper it real low.

It's the perfect word to use,
and real soon I'm sure you'll know.

You too may get hooked on using this new word,
Or perhaps create another to make your feelings heard.

(Instructions: make up some words and tell what you think they mean to you.)

_____

_____

_____

_____

_____

_____

Who's Silly?

My name is Stosh,
and I don't like squash.

I like playing jokes
and the occasional hoax.

I'll demonstrate that now
Are you curious how?

Well, I'll start with a clue
before fooling you.

While my Mom writes this poem pretending to be me,
I'll start my prank, and then you will see.

Somehow she knows just what to say,
she knows me so well, I'm easy to play.

When it's dinnertime and I don't want to eat,
she tells me it's something else, not meat.

She tries to trick me into thinking I'm eating gross things,
like spider legs, mushy brains, even bat wings.

She knows I enjoy things that are gross,
so sometimes she tells me it's eyeball of ghosts.

But I know she's teasing, she can't fool me anymore,
I know her too well, and there's one thing for sure

Those gross things, she would not touch,
but I go along with her pranks and such.

I pretend to enjoy the ears of bat.
She pretends to be happy about that.

So, you think she's pretty silly -- well, is that true?
Maybe she is, but not as silly as you!

I can prove that in one small way
she's probably already fooled you today.

How, you ask?   When you've never even met?
Well, you are simply the silliest one yet!

You think I am me?
Well, let's see

I gave you a clue when I began this rhyme --
My Mom has been writing this whole silly time!

(And you thought it was me!)

Dangling

Some days are lazier than others --
That's when I like to just dangle around.

Some days are easier to handle
When my feet never touch the ground.

Do you have days when you like to dangle
So you just feel that feeling of 'free?'

Do you have days that you have to make better?
Do you have those days, like me?

Write some reasons why you have those days...

_____

_____

_____

Fireworks

Angel dust is falling from above --

It's gently showering me with love.

Fascinating colors bursting with light

As angel dust makes its descending flight.

The thundering noise is a symphony

Booming with passion, just for me.

It's as if

All of my loved ones that have passed away

Have been busy rehearsing all this day.

To make certain with all their might

That I would enjoy this show tonight.

So, there should be no wonder why

When I watch fireworks light up the sky,

No matter how very hard I try,

I smile all the while, and I also cry.

Different

People say my friend is different
Because he's rather tall.
People say my friend is different,
But I don't think so at all.

People say my neighbor's different
Because she's speech impaired.
People say my sister's different
'Cause she has purple hair.

Different means not being the same
Well, I guess 'Different' should be my name!

(Instructions: finish this poem)

I'm different because: _____

_____

_____

_____

Ideas:

Here's how I'm different:

I like to _____

My favorite _____

I eat _____

I read _____

I think it's fun to _____

_____

_____

Almost Zero

I said something today
But no one heard.
I said something today
But it wasn't a word.
I spoke so softly
I barely made a sound.
It wasn't detected
By anyone around.
If I said something important
I could have been a hero.
But when I spoke
It was almost at zero.

So no one heard what I said.
No one could know what it meant.
No one knows I spoke.
The sound came and it went...
Unnoticed it was...
Undetected too.
Unheard by me,
And unheard by you!

Garble

Did you
flibber the glibber
  or
gobble the bobble?

Who would
smiggle the figgle
while
thortin the hortin?

Why'd they
twirtle the birtle
  and
swarble the garble?

I don't understand
it's just making me tense,
this whole thing
doesn't make any sense!

(Instructions: use this space to have some fun making up your own words.)

I'm Late

I'm late, I'm late,

Oh, I hope they wait!

I'm running and hurrying,

I sure hope they're not worrying.

Ugh, if I missed that bus,

That would surely create a fuss.

I really don't want to make a scene,

I told them I'd be there at 3:15.

I'm having such a frazzled Monday!

What's that you say?   It's only Sunday?!

Then why am I racing? I should slow down instead.

Perhaps I'll go back home and _____

_____

_____

_____

(Instructions: finish this poem)

45

Get to Bed

Get to bed at a decent hour
That's what my parents say.
You must wake up bright-eyed and bushy-tailed
That's how you should begin your day.

But I know better, you too will see
'Cause tonight I'll stay up late.
Then, in the morning I'll prove them wrong
Oh boy ...Just you wait!

They've put me to bed, but I'll stay up all night
While they think that I'm asleep.
And then, the joke will be on them
When the first bit of morning light peeks.

My eyes may be a little heavy,
And I just don't feel quite right.
But I'll be up and laughing
At the first sign of morning light!

Hey, what was that noise?
I heard a bang.
Could it be a four-eyed monster
With a big old drippy fang?

Things aren't working out so right,
Somehow I thought this would be fun.
But I know that I'll be better
When I see that rising sun.

Oh-oh, I heard another noise

I think it was Dad ... I'll act like I'm just fine.

What's that he's saying?

'Wake up? ... It's time to rise and shine?'

Wait, what's he doing up now?

I thought it was the middle of the night.

I must have fallen asleep somehow,

What's that I see?   Sunlight?!

Ooohh, who filled my head with cement

And my eyes with sand?

I can barely lift my head

Just to see my hand!

I feel like a three-day old mud pie

That someone threw in a sewer grate.

But, hey, I can't let my folks know

I'll act like I'm just great!

If only I could get up

So they can see I haven't lied

When I told them I don't need much sleep

To wake up bright-tailed and bushy-eyed.

Hmm, something didn't sound quite right there.

I think I made a blunder.

I'll just ponder it a little longer

While I pull up the blanket and crawl back under.

Gramma

I remember my Gramma
from when I was young.
I remember my Gramma
and boy, was she fun!

We'd eat bowls of ice cream
when we really shouldn't.
And she'd help me do things
I normally couldn't.

She'd 'feed' my piggy bank
till it could eat no more.
Then help me spend it
at the toy store.

She'd make me giggle
when I shoulda been asleep.
She gave me lots
of memories to keep.

Now I keep those memories
for us both in store.
'Cause she can't remember
much for herself anymore.

Now, when I visit Gramma
she seems like a child.
And her feisty character
is a little too mild.

But I see a twinkle in her eye
whenever I start
To stir up a memory
that lives in her heart.

A twinkle may not seem
like much to hold.
But it's how I know
I've touched her soul.

And all I really want to do
is pass that twinkle on to you.

(Instructions: write something about your gramma or grampa or someone else special to you)

Flowers, Morsels and Muck

Our home contains all of our 'stuff'
Some frillies, and even the 'rough.'

Things that we do can create muck galore
But the flowers around mean so much more.

There's good and bad in every day
Yet we must decide to make our own way.

If we take in the good, more good will come.
Do we call it a morsel, or do we call it a crumb?

Crumbs are scraps, morsels are to savor.
Choose to taste the morsel's flavor.

Grab the morsels, though muck is abound,
'Cause wonderful things are all around.

Like...

Comfort food smells and playful laughter,
Movies to watch, a dog to chase after,
Video games to drive you crazy,
Long mornings in PJ's just to be lazy,
Good furniture, not to mess up every day,
The play room that's supposed to look that way,
Sled riding until you have a frozen nose,
Hot chocolate that warms you down to your toes,
Jumping off furniture with super powers,
Not to knock over wildly arranged flowers.

You see...

Life is mixed like the things in our home,
Muck and flowers are what we own.

If we see the flowers instead of the muck
Mom says we'll never be stuck.

We'll always be happy with what we do
When we decide to make our own view.

Amid all the muck in our daily routine,
The flowers are always there to be seen.

So, notice the flowers, make the right choice,
And listen to the happier voice.

Be sure to look around, and don't be mistaken
Morsels are there, they're there for the takin!

I Don't Care

I don't care if you care,

I don't need to be knowin'

I don't have to know it

You don't have to show it

'Cause I don't care if you care

I don't need to be knowin'

I don't care if you love me

Hey, where ya goin? . . .

Flying

Oh, how I love to fly --
Way, way up in the clear blue sky.

With the sun on my face
And the wind in my hair,
I soar above clouds
Way up in the air.

With arms open wide,
Sunbeams stream by.
Freely, I glide
And fly through the sky.

I swoop and I dip
And I do a back flip.
I'm flying, I'm flying
Oh, what a fun trip!

Fun to go east, west, north and south
Fun... 'till a bug flies into my mouth!

Sad

I'm feeling rather sad today,
But I'm told that that's OK.

My friend is leaving, it hurts inside.
I know I'm not smiling, but really, I've tried.

I can't help feeling sad, you see,
And, although I'm told I'm allowed to be,

I'd rather just be happy like I think I should,
I'd look on the positive side, if only I could.

But there isn't a positive side to be seen,
Instead, I'm just gloomy, I'm sad & I'm mean.

I'm just feeling rather sad today,
And I guess, after all, that's OK.
Because tomorrow is another day!

(Instructions: have you ever had a friend move away? Or have you ever moved?
If so, write your feelings about it.)

_____

_____

_____

_____

_____

_____

_____

If I Were a Dolphin

If I were a dolphin,

I'd swim all day

And frolic in the ocean blue.

If I were a dolphin,

I'd dance on the water

And have so much fun with you.

If I were a dolphin,

I'd dive way down

Beneath the deep blue sea.

If I were a dolphin,

I'd twirl and spin

And whirl you around with me.

If I were a dolphin,

I'd leap and jump

And make splashes in the sun.

If I were a dolphin,

I'd play all day

And _____

_____

_____

(Instruction: finish this poem)

56

Inflimus Redumius

Inflimus Redumius,
What do these two words mean?

Inflimus Redumius,
Depends on how they're seen.

My one friend thinks
They are angry words.

Another says it's
A species of birds.

My teacher says they are
More intellectual than that.

My bus partner says it's
The name of a bat.

In your mind's eye, what does Inflimus Redumius create?
Finish this poem and draw a picture to relate.

_____

_____

_____

Jump

I jump up and I jump down I jump all around the town with a wiggle and a jiggle a bump and a giggle I jump up and I jump down I jump all around the town.

My Brother

My brother says I make noise when I eat --
But at least my breath doesn't smell like my feet!

My brother says I make messes all over the place --
But at least I don't scare people when they look at my face!

My brother says I'm rude, and he thinks I'm lazy --
But I don't care what he thinks ... I think he's crazy!

My brother says being mean is absurd --
But I don't understand, I'm always nice to that nerd!

My brother says we just don't get along --
But I don't know what he means, I think he's wrong!

My brother says we should be kind and have fun together --
But I think we're fine ... I'm not mean to him ... ever!!!

Snortin' Norton

Snortin' Norton,
That's my dog.

Eats like a pig,
Sounds like a hog.

Snortin' Norton,
Sometimes he stinks.

Sure do wish I knew
What he thinks.

Snortin' Norton,
Even got fleas.

But his tail is a waggin'
And he's eager to please!

Snortin' Norton,
Doesn't seem very smart.

And he makes lazy
Seem like an art.

You might not think
He sounds very fine.

But of all that he is,
I'm sure glad he's mine!

(Instructions: do you have a pet?

If so, write about him or her and draw a picture..

If not, would you like one?

What would he or she look like?)

_____

_____

_____

_____

_____

Night Sky

The sky is rather eerie tonight.
The moon is covered with clouds ... oh, what a sight!

It's casting **long**, spooky shadows outside.
I'd rather just peek at it from here, inside.

Yet, somehow ... so far away in the sky,
While the moon shines down from way up high --

It actually looks kind of small,
And maybe, perhaps, not that eerie at all.

In fact, it moved out from the clouds now and is shining so bright
It really is quite an amazing sight

I've come to believe it's a rather beautiful night
I think I'll sit on the porch for a while and write.

(Instructions: finish writing about the night sky)

_____

_____

_____

_____

_____

_____

_____

Saturday

It's Saturday morning and I could sleep in,
But for some reason, I'm up at dawn.

By 10 a.m. it seems I've been up all day,
Yet, I still have my PJ's on!

The cartoons are really funny,
And I can't stop gigglin' real loud.

If I were anywhere else, I'm sure
I'd be drawing a really big crowd!

My family thinks I'm crazy,
And they tease me about my hair.

I know I've still got 'bed head,'
But I don't really care!

I've already eaten breakfast three times,
And yes, my hair is truly a mess

I hope no one comes a callin'
'Cause I still haven't taken the time to dress!

You see, there's something really cozy
About breaking my weekly routine.

It's Saturday morning, I'm doing my own thing,
And I really shouldn't be seen!

Oh, I do love Saturdays and just being me,
Much different than when I am in school.

Good thing my friends don't see me like this,
Or they surely would NOT think I'm cool!

(Challenge: stand on your head and draw what you see!)

Upside Down

Right side up, upside down.
When my head is down here,
the whole world's turned around!

What was on the floor
is now on the ceiling.
I kinda like this flip-flop feeling.

Nothing's where it should be,
but it's all still in place.
Is this what it's like
to be in outer space?

The world looks so different,
and my head feels rather light,
But, when my feet and head trade places,
things are back to upside right!

Although I feel slightly woozy
from standing on my head,
and some people say it's crazy --
well ... I'm liking it instead.

Perhaps if you try it you too will see
that you like this flip-flop feeling,
just like me!

Somersault

Sometimes I fumble,

Sometimes I bumble,

But mostly I just like to tumble.

I tuck in my chin

And then I begin

To roll over, head over shin.

I spin and I roll

'Till I'm out of control

That's when I'm satisfied down to my soul.

Then when I stop

My head goes "klabop"

And when I try to stand I simply flop!

It's a crazy feeling

That sends me reeling

But somehow it's kind of healing.

Give it a try

Then you'll know why

Somersaults make me laugh till I cry!

Try doing somersaults until you can't stop laughing!

Waiting...

"Just one minute
I forgot my purse."

So, I wait and I wait...
What could be worse?

How much longer?
I can't stand much more.

It seems like hours since
she went through the door.

I pace and I dance while anticipating.
Oh, how I hate the torture of waiting.

I'm waiting patiently
well, maybe not,

But I'm waiting
I'm waiting, and that's all I've got.

I tap my toe
to the beat inside my head,

I'm waiting, I'm waiting,
and I'm filled with dread.

What do you do when you wait?
Do you sit quietly?

I've tried and I've tried
It's not possible for me.

So, I choose a rhythm
and start to hum,

Then I pick up the beat
with an imaginary drum

As I entertain a pretend crowd
I begin singing every word very loud.

Totally engrossed
and singing off key

Proudly, I finish.
Yep, proudly, That's me!

That's when I hear a voice
louder than my own,

"What's going on?"
she asks in that tone!

I'm ready, I'm waiting
"Still waiting!" I yell.

I'm ready, are you?
Oh no, that's just swell!

"Get ready." I was told.
So, ready I got.

I'm ready all ready. Are you?
No, you're not!

I'm bundled and ready
I'm tapping my toe

I'm not happy,
but I'm ready to go.

It's been hours
I've waited hours, I'm sure!

I just can't wait!
Not one minute more!

Then she returns
with purse in hand

70

Glaring.
Staring.
Not a pleasing stand.

"Two minutes,"
she said is all she took

And couldn't I busy myself
with a book?

A book?
A book?
I'd need a book STORE !
Waiting so long,
too long for sure!

So, we get to the mall
yes, finally!

And I'm in the toy store
happy as can be.

They let me try
the new RC car

With newly charged battery,
it will go far!

Mom has to go to a
different store,

But she says she'll wait
just a little while more.

Then she leaves me to play
as she goes to shop
She didn't want to
make me stop.

So, she shopped and shopped,
And when she finally stopped,

She found me still playing
with the same car.

They were right, you know,
it did go really far.

It went so long,
the battery finally died,

And my poor brain
was completely fried.

I didn't realize just how long
Mom waited and waited
without a whining song.

Then it hit me
that I had been waiting, too
while she shopped the mall!

But it wasn't so bad while I played,
not bad at all!

I guess waiting is really
no big deal,

If only I didn't
act like a heel!

Word Games:

Take one or more words from each column below and use those words to write a poem or, use the Origami pages in back of the book or, make up your own list of words and use them to write a poem. Be creative, be silly, have fun!

1	2	3
Red	Doodletooth	Schnickerschnarppened
Yellow	Cuddlecrumface	Flipperflodding
Blue	Lililobe	Clammerblooed
Green	Barterbuglebum	Imberclawing
Orange	Finklehead	Voddlemuked
Purple	Plunkerfoot	Bulbertooning
Pink	Toobernose	Quintelquoping
White	Goobymcfloobylips	Nuskitwigging
Black	Knarlyknees	Limberlooned
Brown	Wuggychumberarm	Zungercrumpled
Indigo	Himberleg	Wogelframed
Aqua	Snogglefinger	Krinklecrowed
Crimson	Mumbletoe	Angletoomed
Burgundy	Zungertooplehand	Pickerputting
Chestnut	Artichokebelly	Morpeltwisting
Rose	Jabberjimakajaw	Twinkledinked
Coral	Ibbereye	Jongeryecked
Peach	Rankleankle	Dablospelling
Turquoise	Vondleromychin	Yemmaglassing
Magenta	Eaglevonpuckerear	Roverfreshed
Violet	Niddlemcfiddleshin	Gigglehooking
Emerald	Oshmowelbow	Ubersonged
Gray	Quizinbuttonknuckle	Ebbystrayed
Periwinkle	Underputpalm	Orbilfratting
Teal	Yinkleyamcheek	Hinglebopped

72

Origami Poetry Writer

Follow these easy instructions to make your own Origami Poetry Writer.

First, you will need the following supplies:

Sheet of paper (plain)

Scissors

Pencil or pen

List of words (on Page 72, or make up your own!)

1.

- If your paper is not perfectly square, begin by folding a corner of the paper over the other side (to make a triangle).

- Then cut off the excess portion.

- Note: if your paper is already perfectly square, skip the steps above, and just fold it into a triangle.

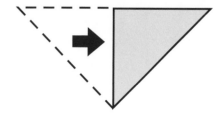

2.

- Now we have to crease the paper so that it will work easily as an Origami Poetry Writer.

- So, fold the triangle in half to make a smaller triangle.

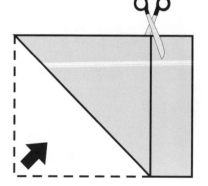

3.

- Then unfold all the folds until the paper is back to being a big square.

- And fold all 4 corners in (bringing the points to the center of the paper) until you have a smaller square.

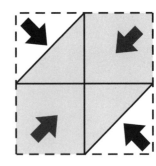

4.

- Flip the paper over.

- And fold the new corners in (bringing the points to the center of the paper) until you have an even smaller square.

- Note: Do not flip over.

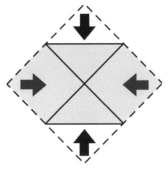

5.

- Now fold the square in half (forming a rectangle) to crease the paper.

- Unfold it and fold it in half (forming a rectangle) to crease the paper the other way.

6.

- Unfold it again and fold it in half, bringing 2 points together (forming a triangle) to crease the paper.

- Unfold it and fold it in half, bringing the other 2 points together (forming a triangle) to crease the paper the other way.

- Note: Your Origami Poetry Writer is almost ready....

- Slip it over your fingers to see how it works.

- Notice the 4 outside flaps that your fingers are under.

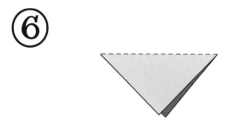

7.

- Now lay the Origami down so those 4 flaps are facing up.

- Write a color (from Page 72, column 1, or choose your own) on each of the 4 flaps.

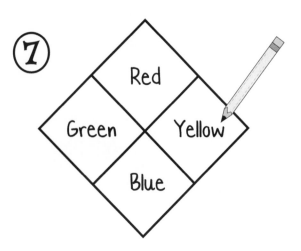

8.

 • Flip it over and write a word (from Page 72, column 2, or make up your own) on each section of the flaps (total of 8 words).

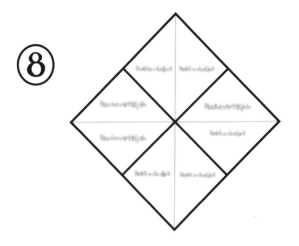

9.

 • Open the flaps and write a word (from Page 72 column 3, or make up your own) on the underside of each of the 4 flaps

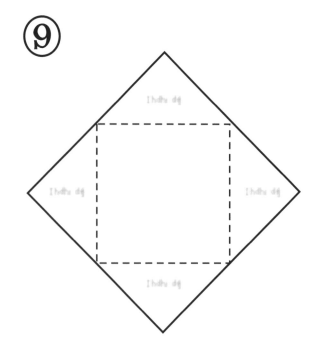

10.

- Refold to close the flaps and bring all the points together (so only the colors show on the outside) and place your fingers under the color flaps.

Now your Origami Poetry Writer is completed and ready to use!

Here's how you use it to write a poem:

Choose a color and write that color down on a new sheet of paper.

With 4 fingers under the color flaps, move the Origami Poetry Writer around with your fingers (opening and closing it) while you spell out the color you chose.

Now, wherever you stopped (while spelling your color) you should see 4 words inside the Origami Poetry Writer, choose one of those words and write it down on the sheet of paper (with the color you picked).

After you write down that word, pick up the flap to see what word is underneath (on the inside of the Origami Poetry Writer) and write that word down with the other two words.
Now, use the 3 words you have written down to write a poem...remember, it does not have to rhyme.
It can be silly, serious, long or short. There are no rules.

Just use your imagination and write, write, WRITE!

please visit
www.colormyworld.info

About The Author

Photography by Robert Strovers

Debbie Mancini-Wilson is a native of Pittsburgh, Pennsylvania who enjoys the rousing beauty of the city, along with its intellectual and cultural diversities, and the abundance of ethnic foods and ways of life. A writer truly could not ask for a more stimulating place to live! You can frequently find Debbie shopping in the city's open market for all the flavors of Pittsburgh. However, it is at home where she is most comfortable cooking for and entertaining family and friends. She currently lives in a suburb north of the city with her husband (Dana), their two sons (Stefan and Josh), and their dog (Sparky) … all of whom inspired most of the poems in this book.